STRESSED-OUT GIRL?

Girls Dealing With Feelings

Annie Belfield

JASMINE
H E A L T H
Wellness • Diet • Cooking

Jasmine Health, an imprint of Enslow Publishers, Inc.

Library of Congress Cataloging-in-Publication Data

Belfield, Annie.
 [A girls' guide to stress]
 Stressed-out girl? : girls dealing with feelings / Annie Belfield.
  pages cm. — (Girls dealing with feelings)
 Originally published in 2008 as A Girls' Guide to Stress."
 Includes bibliographical references and index.
 Summary: "Explores the emotion of stress in young women and the best ways to deal with it and the situations that cause it. Includes real-life examples, quotes, facts, tips, and quizzes"—Provided by publisher.
 ISBN 978-1-62293-040-1 — ISBN 978-1-62293-041-8 (pbk) — ISBN 978-1-62293-042-5 (ePUB) — ISBN 978-1-62293-043-2 (PDF) — ISBN 978-1-62293-044-9 (PDF) 1. Stress (Psychology). 2. Girls—Life skills guides. I. Title.
 BF575.S75B376 2014
 155.5'33—dc23
                      2013015766
Future editions:
Paperback ISBN: 978-1-62293-041-8   EPUB ISBN: 978-1-62293-042-5
Single-User PDF ISBN: 978-1-62293-043-2   Multi-User PDF ISBN: 978-1-62293-044-9

Printed in the United States of America
072014 HF Group, North Manchester, IN
10 9 8 7 6 5 4 3 2 1

To Our Readers: We have done our best to make sure all Internet addresses in this book were active and appropriate when we went to press. However, the author and the publisher have no control over and assume no liability for the material available on those Internet sites or on other Web sites they may link to. Any comments or suggestions can be sent by e-mail to comments@enslow.com or to the address below.

Jasmine Health
Box 398, 40 Industrial Road
Berkeley Heights, NJ 07922
USA
www.jasminehealth.com

Illustration Credits: Shutterstock.com: Cory Thoman (brainstorm graphic), pp. 19, 46; freesoulproduction (thumbtack graphic), pp. 6, 7, 11, 13, 14, 16, 18, 32, 47, 51, 52, 55; NLshop (therapist graphic), pp. 23, 26, 27, 34, 38, 44, 57, 60, 61; Seamartini Graphics (atom graphic), pp. 16, 25, 30, 36, 39; vectorgirl (lightbulb graphic), pp. 10, 56; wavebreakmedia/Shutterstock.com, p. 1; zayats-and-zayats (quotation graphic), pp. 9, 21.

Cover Photo: wavebreakmedia/Shutterstock.com

This book was originally published in 2008 as A Girls' Guide to Stress.

CONTENTS

CHAPTER ONE

What Is Stress?

> Zoe sat nervously at her desk, tapping her pencil and chewing on her hair. The math final was today, and even though she had studied really hard, she just didn't get it. If she didn't do well, her parents said she was going to be grounded for a month. It wasn't fair.

On the day of a major exam in just about any class, you're likely to see signs of nervousness. Kids are frantically looking over their notes, biting their nails, chewing their pencil erasers, cracking their knuckles, or taking deep breaths.

In fact, you may be doing the same thing. That nervous, jittery feeling you are having is called stress. Its source—the test—is your stressor. Even if you usually feel confident during tests, odds are you've experienced stress in other situations.

Stress is a normal part of life. It's your body's emotional reaction to everything urgent, exciting, frightening, irritating, or significant. Depending on the situation, stress can occur when you are overly excited about something, mad at somebody or some situation, running scared, or anticipating being embarrassed or ashamed.

Stress can be positive when it pushes you to do your best at a task. For example, it can give you the mental alertness you need to do well in a major test. Or it can give you that extra physical energy in a race that propels you first across the finish line. However, stress can also be bad for you. When you have too much stress—and it lasts over a long period of time— you can feel overwhelmed and helpless. People often describe such feelings as being "stressed out."

Has someone ever implied that your stress isn't important because of your age? Well-meaning adults don't always get it. You probably don't work full-time, pay taxes, or have anyone who depends on you for everything. Some adults may think this means you have no real problems. They only remember the fun times of when they were young and have forgotten the miserable moments. At this stage of life, you may be faced with difficult situations that would overwhelm anybody.

Stress isn't the most enjoyable emotion, but it's not necessarily a cause for panic. The key is learning to handle your stress in a healthy way so you can control it, live with it, and maybe even benefit from it occasionally. Knowing what to expect and how to cope will help you deal with common stressors.

This book gives specific strategies and solutions to help you understand and manage your own stress. It includes information on how people respond—in good ways and unhealthy ways—to stressful situations. It also describes common stressors—family, friends, school, and life in general—and suggests ways to manage them.

Signs of Teen Stress

1. Feeling down, on edge, guilty, or tired
2. Having headaches, stomachaches, or trouble sleeping
3. Wanting to be alone all the time
4. Not enjoying activities you used to enjoy
5. Feeling resentful of others
6. Feeling like you have too many things you have to do

Common Stressors

Family trouble: divorced, separated, or remarrying parents; pushy parents who expect too much; different priorities from family members; competition with siblings.

Issues with friends: arguments; mean and catty behavior during difficult times; getting trapped in the middle of group fights; friends who need urgent help.

Academic and social aspects of school: making friends, especially when new to the neighborhood; pressure to get top grades; increasingly difficult tests and projects; too much homework; bullies.

Insecurity with self: the urge to be the best at everything; negative body image.

Change in general: new settings; loss or illness of loved ones; growing apart from friends.

CHAPTER TWO

How Your Body Reacts

Did you know that the emotions associated with stress actually cause physical changes in your body? A Hungarian scientist and physician named Hans Selye identified this response in 1936 while experimenting on mice. Although he injected the animals with various kinds of fluids, they all developed ulcers, swelling glands, and depleted immune systems. (The body's immune system helps fight infection.) The mice's bodies changed, or adapted, in the same way.

Selye called this response general adaptation syndrome. Later, as he expanded his work on general adaptation syndrome, he began referring to it as *stress*. At the time, physicists used the term, which comes from a Latin word meaning "to pull apart," to describe elasticity.

According to a colleague of Selye's, the word *strain* was closer to the idea of what the researcher was trying to describe. (*Strain* refers to an injury to the body caused by extreme physical tension.) If Selye had been more proficient in English, people today might be talking about "strain relief" instead of "stress relief"! But the name *stress* stuck, and others began researching the subject as well.

So exactly how does stress affect people? Actually, it's all in your head—more specifically, in your brain. The physical reaction to stress is triggered by a part of your brain called the hypothalamus. Although the hypothalamus is only about the size of a marble, it affects your entire body. This tiny region of the brain is a control center that sparks many complex

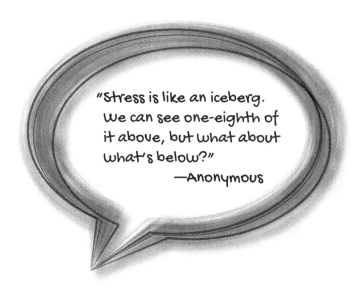

"Stress is like an iceberg. We can see one-eighth of it above, but what about what's below?"
—Anonymous

Adrenaline and Cortisol

Adrenaline and cortisol are produced by the adrenal glands—two boomerang-shaped glands located near your kidneys. Adrenaline increases the heart rate and raises your blood pressure. Cortisol regulates metabolism, which is the process in which the body breaks down substances so the cells can use them. Both adrenaline and cortisol increase the amount of sugar in the bloodstream, which results in feeling a rush of energy.

chemical reactions. Among them is the release of hormones—special chemical substances that signal other body cells to action. In emergency situations, the hypothalamus sets off an alarm resulting in the release of two important hormones—adrenaline and cortisol—into the bloodstream. They cause changes to quickly occur in the body: the muscles tense and breathing becomes rapid.

This stress reaction is called the "fight-or-flight" response—your body is prepared to fight the perceived danger or flee from it. The fight-or-flight instinct is a natural response that dates to prehistoric times, when humans had to struggle for survival.

Although you probably don't have to face mortal danger on a regular basis today, you still experience

Stressed-Out Girl? Girls Dealing With Feelings

fight-or-flight moments. The stress response can occur when your emotions cause your body to react as it would in an actual emergency, even when there is no physical danger.

Once the stressful event or threat that set off your hypothalamus alarm has passed, the levels of adrenaline and cortisol decrease in the bloodstream. Your body returns to normal.

The Power of Adrenaline

You may have been surprised by your own strength or speed in an emergency situation. Chalk it up to the adrenaline rush of your body's stress response. For example, when you stumble on a steep flight of stairs, you don't have to think about reaching out to grab the railing. It just happens in a split second. Stress-induced adrenaline can also sharpen your reflexes and give you a "second wind," delivering a burst of renewed energy that allows you to keep working even when you're tired.

CHAPTER THREE

How Stress Makes You Feel

> *Kayla was nervous. She had practiced her speech for the school assembly over and over again. But as she walked over to the podium, she forgot everything she was going to say. Her heart was pounding, her stomach hurt, and her hands were shaking so much that she couldn't see the words on her note cards.*

You probably are familiar with many of the symptoms of stress. It can cause a number of unpleasant side effects in your body, in your mind, and in the way you behave. There's no reason to be anxious about the symptoms of stress. However, it's important to know what they are. When you have an idea of what to expect, you can recognize when you need to figure out ways to cope.

Physical reactions. Like Kayla, you might exhibit a variety of symptoms when under stress. Your heart beats fast, your breathing becomes heavier, and you sweat. You might feel various aches and pains as your muscles clench up or get tense. If they remain that way for a long time, they may cause pain, especially in the neck, back, and shoulders.

Headaches are often a common response to stress—a result of the increased amount of blood rushing to the brain. At the same time, the digestive system is receiving less blood, so your stomach typically feels queasy. Whenever you're nervous, the stress response can produce a sensation often referred to as "butterflies" in the stomach.

There are two specific types of stress—acute and chronic. Acute stress occurs when the fight-or-flight response is triggered right away. The stressful feeling comes up quickly, is intense, and then disappears

Physical Reactions to Stress

- Headache
- Aching neck and shoulders
- Teeth grinding
- Heartburn
- Shaking legs
- Flushed face
- Dry mouth and throat
- Sweaty hands
- Poor appetite
- Upset stomach or nausea

quickly. Chronic stress, on the other hand, lasts a long time. The body does not return to its natural state but remains in the fight-or-flight response.

If you are exposed to chronic stress, the constant high levels of adrenaline and cortisol in the bloodstream can cause all kinds of problems. Chronic stress weakens the immune system, leaving

Three Stages of Stress

When you are dealing with a stressful situation, your body reacts in three basic stages:

Stage One: The first reaction is called the alarm phase. Your mouth goes dry, your heart pounds, it gets difficult to breathe, you're either sweating or trembling, the pupils of your eyes dilate, and your stomach lurches.

Stage Two: To deal with long-term stress, your body enters the second stage, called the resistance or adaptation stage. Your blood sugar levels and blood pressure rise as your body tries to sustain its heightened energy levels. You may feel anxious or angry.

Stage Three: If a stressor hasn't been successfully dealt with over the long term and the body's stockpile of energy runs out, you reach a third stage, called the exhaustion phase. It is accompanied by feelings of being overwhelmed and tired.

you at greater risk to catch infections and diseases. Symptoms of long-term stress can include insomnia, heart disease, and depression, as well as stomachaches and headaches.

Chronic stress can also be harsh on your skin. If your face breaks out when you're feeling stressed, there's a scientific explanation: the high levels of cortisol in your body are causing skin glands to produce more oil than necessary. Sometimes people under stress suffer from another kind of skin problem, which is slightly more serious but still not usually harmful—hives. These are itchy, swollen welts that can appear anywhere on the body and take up to twenty-four hours to fade away.

During the teen years, the human body undergoes many changes during puberty—the time when kids are maturing into adults. In girls, the hormonal changes associated with puberty (which typically occurs between the ages of eight and thirteen) cause the girl to develop breasts and begin having a menstrual cycle. However, the hormonal changes caused by prolonged stress can make that cycle irregular. After stress levels are lowered, it will return to normal.

Emotional and behavioral reactions. Chronic stress typically affects emotions and behavior. For example, if you're struggling for several months to deal with a bully or your parents' divorce, your low feelings

⚛ ⚛ ⚛ Science Says... ⚛ ⚛ ⚛

A 2007 study released by researchers from Wake Forest University School of Medicine and colleagues found that teens under high levels of stress were 23 percent more likely than other teens to have problems with acne.

Whenever you're stressed out, you can take a few precautions to reduce chances of a breakout: Wash—but don't scrub—your face twice a day. Resist the urge to pop or pick existing zits. If you wear makeup or use facial cleanser, avoid products with isopropyl (rubbing) alcohol or nutshell fragments.

Emotional Reactions to Stress

- Anxiety
- Worrying
- Irritability
- Sadness
- Dissatisfaction

- Anger
- Confusion
- Guilt
- Depression

and mood swings will affect your behavior. You may react to situations without thinking and have a low threshold for tolerating or dealing with challenges. If you are dealing with long-term stress:

- You may be tense, panicky, on edge, and easily startled.
- You may feel like you'll go crazy if one more thing happens.
- Your mind may wander so often you can't concentrate, keep track of time, or make decisions.
- You may find yourself crying for no reason, or getting furious over something that's no big deal.
- Depending on the stressor, you're also likely to feel angry, afraid, or humiliated.
- You may also not feel like doing anything. In fact, you probably wish people would just leave you alone.

Be aware that your low emotions and moods not only affect your actions, but also how others react to you. People undergoing long-term stress often reach a point where they simply don't care what others think of their behavior.

If you're dealing with a long-term stressful situation, you're likely to become preoccupied and distracted. Your parents think you're being rude. Your friends start to wonder why you're giving them the silent

Behavioral Reactions to Stress

- Overeating or undereating
- Angry outbursts
- Substance abuse
- Crying spells
- Conflicts with others
- Decreased ability to get work done

treatment. Because you are having so much difficulty concentrating, you can't focus in class. Your teachers think you're not paying attention, and so your grades suffer. Stress can make your relationships with others become more difficult.

It's important that you recognize when you're stressed out. Then it will be easier to see how your behavior is affecting others. Try to be considerate of others as you attempt to function as normally as possible. For instance, no matter how irritable you're feeling, try not to snap at anyone who shows concern.

Similarly, try to be patient when somebody else's stress is driving you crazy. Keep a low profile when it seems like all your friends are stressed out. In fact, you might want to stay out of everybody's way until things calm down.

How Stressed Are You?

Determine how you react to stress. Count up the number of sentences you agree with. Then evaluate how stressed out you are by using the following score: *6 or more* = *stress level is high;* *2 to 5* = *stress level is average;* *1 or 0* = *stress level is below average.*

1. I often feel tense or anxious.

2. I frequently have stomachaches.

3. My family often makes me feel upset.

4. I get nervous around people at school.

5. I often get headaches.

6. I have trouble falling asleep at night.

7. I worry about school.

8. When I get nervous, I tend to snack.

9. I have trouble concentrating on one thing because I'm worrying about something else.

10. I have considered using drugs or drinking to relax.

11. I have a full schedule of responsibilities at school and at home.

12. I have trouble finding time to relax.

13. I often feel guilty that I'm not doing my homework or other chores.

CHAPTER FOUR

What to Do When You're Stressed

Hurry up—you need to finish this by noon. Is your homework done? Did you practice your music today? I'm mad at you. Did you make the team? Do you know if you got the part? We don't like your friends. Don't you think you should lose some weight? Can't you get better grades? Why didn't you play a better game?

Messages like these can certainly stress you out. This is especially true if you feel that countless demands and pressures are coming at you from all directions: from parents, friends, teachers, coaches, and even yourself. If you are feeling overwhelmed, you can use the following suggestions to cope:

Learn to recognize when stress is affecting you. When you first feel the physical stress response coming on—stiffened muscles or flushed face—recognize you are having a fight-or-flight response. Identify your stressors as well as the emotion or combination of emotions you are feeling.

Put your stressors in perspective. Perspective refers to viewing things according to their importance. Remember, the fight-or-flight response can kick in whenever your emotions make your brain think there is an emergency. Learn to recognize the difference between true emergencies and events that are important, but not life threatening. As Natalie Goldberg, author of *Wild Mind: Living the Writer's Life,* has explained, "Stress is an ignorant state. It believes that everything is an emergency."

You may find that you can calm yourself down (or reduce your stress response) simply by putting the situation in perspective. Say, for example, you failed a history test because you studied the wrong chapter.

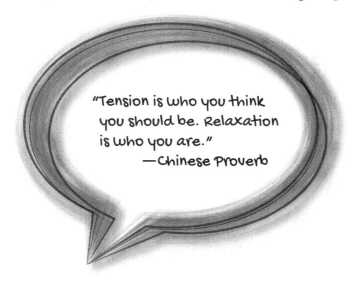

"Tension is who you think you should be. Relaxation is who you are."
—Chinese Proverb

Find out how much of that grade will affect your overall standing. You may learn it will be only a small part, or may not count at all. You could also try talking to your teacher to see if you could take the test again. Rather than get upset, take positive steps to deal with a potential stressor.

Prioritize your obligations. Similarly, if you feel overwhelmed because you have a busy schedule, be willing to make some changes. Evaluate your current schedule. Decide what needs to get done sooner, and what can be finished at a later time. You may find that you have to drop some things, and be willing to do so. Recognize your limitations and set specific goals.

Make large tasks manageable. If you have a large assignment to do, can you find a way to break it down into smaller, more easily achievable tasks? For example, if you have an hour to finish twenty math problems, break down your work in a way that will let you stay on track. One way might be to plan to finish five problems every fifteen minutes.

Be assertive in standing up for yourself. Being assertive means being able to express your feelings, opinions, or beliefs clearly, while respecting the needs and rights of others. You can often bring a stressful situation—with parents, friends, or siblings—to a close when you are assertive. But when dealing with a

Ways to Relieve Stress

1. Spend some time by yourself.

2. Go for a run.

3. Work on your favorite hobby or start a new one.

4. Sing with a group of people.

5. Bake or cook something special.

6. Play a musical instrument or listen to music.

7. Play a sport that you enjoy.

8. Talk to someone who is a good listener.

stressful conflict, be sure to state your feelings calmly and politely.

Take care of yourself emotionally. Take a break when you find yourself in a stressful situation. Walk away when someone is upsetting you, or leave the room to give yourself the chance to "talk yourself down" from your own anger.

Do something to take your mind off your stress. Play your favorite songs—whether they're relaxing, angry, or somewhere in between. Take a shower. Play with your pet. Make faces at yourself in the mirror.

Make yourself laugh by thinking about some joke that never gets old. Some people find that prayer, meditation, yoga, and sleep help them if they are feeling stressed out. Others may use breathing or muscle relaxation techniques such as the ones that appear on pages 26 and 27.

Writing your feelings down in a journal can be a great outlet when you're stressed. Like any negative feeling, stress can seem like less of a big deal once you write about it. A lot of people like to record their actions and verbalize their daily feelings through prose or poetry. Journaling is ideal for when you want to blow off steam but don't feel like talking about what's bothering you to anyone else.

However, sharing your problems with a trusted friend or adult can help. You might also find relief by joining and participating in a support group whose members are dealing with the same stressful issues you have.

Take care of yourself physically. You will be better able to minimize the negative effects of stress if your body is healthy. Three important ways to maintain good health are to eat well, exercise regularly, and get plenty of sleep.

When you're stressed, some foods are more helpful than others. Foods rich in carbohydrates, such as rice, potatoes, pasta, cereal, and bread, can boost energy. The fiber in grains, fruits, and vegetables helps keep the digestive system moving. Such foods can also settle your stomach if stress is making you nauseous. Fried food, on the other hand, can worsen your stomachache.

Regular exercise decreases the production of stress hormones in the body. And physical activity also causes the body to release mood-boosting brain chemicals called endorphins. As a result, exercise will reduce your stressful feelings and make you feel good, too. If it's not possible for you to maintain a regular exercise schedule, try to get moderately strenuous exercise at least twice a week. This could include a short walk, bike ride, or jog.

Get enough sleep whenever you can. Most teenagers need between 8.5 and 9.5 hours per night,

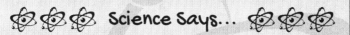

Science Says...

Playing with your pet can reduce stress. Many nursing homes, psychiatric wards, and rehabilitation clinics bring rabbits, cats, or dogs into their facilities so the animals can provide therapy for patients. People who have the opportunity to interact with the animals have reduced blood pressure and feel more positive.

Breathing Relaxation

1. Sit in a comfortable chair, feet flat on the floor.

2. Close your eyes or focus on something in the room.

3. Paying attention to your breathing, inhale slowly through your nose.

4. Let your lower abdomen relax and expand as your lungs expand and fill with air.

5. When your lungs and abdomen are full, slowly exhale, letting air out through your mouth.

6. Repeat. If your mind wanders, return your attention to your breathing.

Adapted from "Breathe Deeply to Manage Stress," *EmaxHealth*, March 18, 2006, www. emaxhealth.com

---

researchers say. However, a large number of teens don't get nearly that much. In a 1997 study, professors from Brown University and College of the Holy Cross found that only 26 percent of surveyed teens regularly slept for 8.5 hours. In other words, almost three quarters of all teens are sleep-deprived. Exhaustion saps concentration, weakens the immune system, and makes existing stress worse.

Muscle Relaxation

1. Work on slowly tensing and then relaxing each muscle group in your body.

2. Begin by tensing and relaxing the muscles in your toes. Then work your way up various muscles in the body until you reach the ones in your neck and head.

3. For each set of muscles, hold the tension for at least five seconds. Then relax for thirty seconds.

4. Repeat until you feel less stressed out.

"Relaxation Techniques: Learn Ways to Calm Your Stress," Mayo Clinic, March 7, 2007

CHAPTER FIVE

Harmful ways of Coping

> As she stomped home from school, Maya grew more and more worried. Her best friend had picked a fight with her for no apparent reason. She wouldn't have much time to study for tomorrow's history test because she had a dentist appointment that afternoon. When she arrived at home, Maya slammed her backpack down and collapsed on the floor.
>
> "How come you're so grumpy?" her little sister asked curiously.
>
> "Why do you care? Mind your own business!" Maya snapped.

f you're stressed, there are many ways you can relieve your tension and anger. But a few approaches to dealing with stress are never helpful, especially if they involve being inconsiderate of others or mistreating your body. Unfortunately, these counterproductive actions can be hard to recognize.

Lashing out, overreacting, or venting. Maya's problem wasn't really with her sister. What she was doing was taking her anger out on someone else who actually had nothing to do with her stressors: her angry friend, her upcoming test, and her tight schedule. It's unfair to lash out at people or other living things. And if your target strikes back, you could find yourself with an even more stressful situation.

Before you snap in anger at someone who has had nothing to do with your problems, try counting to ten. During this time, remind yourself that venting will do nothing to solve your difficulty. It most likely will only create additional problems. If you find that you can't stop from lashing out at others, you may be having issues that would be helped by counseling.

Suppressing, avoiding, or ignoring. Suppressing or ignoring your stressor and hoping it will go away on its own may keep you from panicking. However, the longer you ignore a stressful situation, the more urgent it may become. By not dealing with your stress, you run the risk of having it negatively affect your health over the long term as chronic stress.

Eating too much—or too little. Many people drastically change how they eat when they're stressed out. Some overeat, or binge, on "comfort foods" while others go hungry. Both overeating and undereating can do real harm to your health.

While eating cookies might improve your mood because of the short-term effect of additional sugar in your bloodstream, the "sugar rush" won't last long. Be aware that eating in response to your emotions—rather than simply in response to the hunger drive—can lead to serious eating disorders. Overeating can also cause health problems such as being overweight or obese.

And don't skip meals because you're stressed out. Make sure you eat three balanced meals a day of nutritious foods. Even if you lose your appetite or feel queasy because you're anxious, keep yourself healthy by eating properly—even if you can't eat very much.

⚛ ⚛ ⚛ Science Says… ⚛ ⚛ ⚛

Carbohydrates in foods such as sweets, potato chips, and bread cause a temporary increase in serotonin, a brain chemical that affects emotions, memory, and other things. Increased amounts of serotonin in the brain make people feel good, so they think they can better handle stress. Because of this, some people will respond to stressful situations by overeating foods that are rich in carbohydrates.

Using alcohol and illegal substances. In some cases, people try to escape from their problems by using alcohol, nicotine, and drugs, including illegal substances. Using artificial means to deal with stressful situations won't help solve problems. They often tend to create new ones. Substance abuse is habit-forming, and it is easy to become addicted to alcohol and drugs.

You may have heard that people are more cheerful and playful while drinking, but appearing cheerful and actually being happy can be two different things. Alcohol is actually a depressant, which is a kind of drug that calms nerves and relaxes the muscles. However, in large amounts depressants can cause confusion, lack of coordination, slurred speech, and shaking. Mood swings are common with heavy drinkers, who are just as likely to feel gloomy or aggressive as a stressed out person who isn't drinking. Because the use of alcohol is illegal for anyone under the age of twenty-one, getting caught using it can also lead to problems with the law. You definitely don't want that kind of stress.

You're also likely to have heard that smoking cigarettes calms the nerves. But the exact opposite is true: when a smoker lights up, adrenaline is released into his or her system. Even if nicotine really did have a calming effect, this benefit still wouldn't be worth the risks. Not only is nicotine use addictive, but its long-term use has been linked to serious lung diseases such as emphysema and lung cancer.

Another unhealthy way of dealing with stress is using illegal substances such as marijuana. Its active ingredient, THC (delta-9-tetrahydrocannabinol), induces relaxation when it reacts with substances in the brain. But marijuana is an illegal drug whose use has been linked to numerous adverse effects, including short-term memory loss.

There are many healthy ways to deal with stress. Using alcohol, tobacco, or other drugs to cope is not one of them.

Problems With Caffeine

The world's most commonly used drug, caffeine is a stimulant found in foods like coffee, tea, chocolate, and sodas. Millions of people start their day each morning by drinking caffeine. It affects the nervous system (the brain, spinal cord, and nerves) and energizes the body. However, caffeine is a drug and it is possible to have too much at once or to become dependent on it. Consuming even a moderate amount of caffeine can affect your sleeping patterns and cause headaches and muscle pains.

CHAPTER SIX

Stressed Out by Family

Most parents love their kids and want the best for them. But without meaning to, they can pile on unreasonable amounts of pressure to get top grades, win an athletic scholarship, or be one of the popular kids. It is easy for teens to feel stress when parents make them feel like their best just isn't good enough.

Just remember, your parents really do have your best interests in mind. But if you are upset by their expectations, you need to tell them what you're feeling and what it is that you want. Similarly, if you think they don't treat you fairly in other ways, talk to them.

In any conversation you have with adults, make your case quietly and calmly. Then, listen to and honestly consider their response. Don't sigh or roll your eyes, no matter what they say. Your parents may not agree with you or change their minds, but they'll probably be impressed by your maturity. As a result, you may be able to reach a compromise.

Tips for Talking with Your Parents

1. When your parents say something that makes you angry or tense, don't confront them while emotions are running high. Excuse yourself and take some time to cool off.

2. Give yourself a little while to gather and organize your thoughts. What exactly do you want them to know? You might want to write your arguments down in a list.

3. After figuring out what you'd like to say, ask to speak with your parents.

4. Be levelheaded and avoid exaggeration; they should be more likely to consider your points if you present them calmly.

If it seems like your parents expect you to be perfect or don't respect your uniqueness, you shouldn't accept this kind of pressure. Tell them you need them to change their way of thinking because it is hurting you.

In the same way, don't get stressed out by conflicts with brothers and sisters. When siblings tease or misbehave, keep your cool. Talk out your issues calmly, following the same suggestions given above for talking with parents.

CHAPTER SEVEN

Stressed Out by Friends

Your good friend Nicole just came crying to you. She says that Shannon had asked out Ben, Nicole's ex-boyfriend, just to be mean. An hour later, Shannon furiously tells you that Ben had asked her out—not the other way around. She says that Nicole's spreading lies because she's jealous.

You really don't want to get involved, but you realize that both your friends expect you to pick a side. If you defend one, the other will get mad at you, and if you ignore the whole thing, they'll both get mad at you! Suddenly, you're stressing out over an issue that otherwise wouldn't affect your life at all.

Friends. You'd trust them with your life, and they've heard stuff you'd never consider telling anyone else. When something terrible happens, your first instinct is to call them. But when friends know all each other's secrets and quirks, they're able to hurt each other like no one else can. Your friends can be great at helping you deal with stress. Other times, friends are the stressors.

When friends involve you in their conflicts. It's hard to know how to react when other people impose their problems on you. Sure, it's not fair when others expect you to get involved in a conflict you're not part of. And it can be difficult to know what to do when you constantly have to hear about someone else's personal issues. It may be tempting to yell "Will you just shut up already about Nicole and your stupid boyfriend? Why do you think I care?" Needless to say, venting like that will only make everyone involved even angrier.

However, you could take a more tactful approach by being assertive and calmly stating your point of view. "Shannon," you could say, "I'm sorry about this fight, but it's between you and Nicole, and nobody else. I can't judge whose fault it is—and frankly, I don't really want to. Let me know if I can help, but

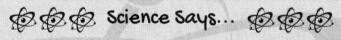 Science Says...

A University of Pittsburgh study found that among people subjected to stressful laboratory experiments, those who were accompanied by friends had lower heart rates and lower blood pressure than those who came alone. In other words, supportive friends reduce stress.

otherwise, can we just not talk about it?" Even if such a response annoys your friends at first, it lets them know where they stand. They'll probably work out their conflict on their own. And in the meantime, you won't be stressed out by it.

When you have conflicts with friends. All friends fight. And conflict can be stressful. You may wonder, "Will we ever be friends again? Will she tell the whole school my secrets? What if everybody else sides with her and I lose all my other friends?" In addition to those worries, you may be flooded by emotions of anger, betrayal, and humiliation. It may seem like your whole world is collapsing.

Sometimes you just can't avoid getting into an argument. However, you can learn ways to deal with conflicts so they end quickly and are less stressful for all involved. Remember, when fighting breaks out, keep your comments fair and civil. More tips for resolving conflict appear on page 38. These tips apply to fights with family members, too.

Dealing with peer pressure. Friends can be a stressor in another way—when they push you to behave in a way that you're not comfortable. It can be particularly stressful when your peers—the people who are your age—pressure you into making bad choices. Peer pressure can lead to bad decision-

Tips for Resolving Conflicts

Do: Explain your reasons carefully. Saying "I was upset when . . ." is friendlier than accusing with a statement like "You upset me when . . . "

Do: Listen quietly while the other person is speaking. Instead of interrupting, shouting down, or deliberately ignoring the other person, wait your turn.

Do: Accept responsibility for your role in the argument, even if you've been treated poorly. Fights are rarely just one person's fault.

Do: Remember that one argument doesn't doom a friendship. If you spend a lot of time with someone, it is natural that you'll disagree on occasion.

Don't: Spread gossip. Not only is it unkind, it often just makes things worse.

Don't: Use blanket statements like "You're always late," or "You've never cared about anyone but yourself!" Words like always, whenever, and never are dangerous when used in statements accusing others.

Don't: Complicate things and make the conflict worse by bringing up old arguments, making personal attacks, or attempting revenge.

Don't: Be afraid to apologize first. Even if the argument wasn't your fault, that doesn't matter. What really matters is ending the conflict.

making, especially when it comes to the use of drugs, alcohol, or tobacco.

It can be stressful when you find yourself going against the wishes of the group, especially if you want to be liked or to fit in. However, when you know something is wrong for you, let the group know. You might try talking to just one member of the crowd. Perhaps you can get her to agree with your way of thinking. Having the support of one other person can make it easier for you to resist the pressure to do something you believe is wrong.

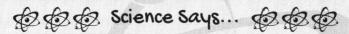

⚛ ⚛ ⚛ Science Says... ⚛ ⚛ ⚛

Sometimes laughter is the best medicine. Studies indicate that regular exposure to humor and laughter reduces stress, anxiety, and tension. Researchers at Loma Linda University in California found that laughter decreases the release of two stress-related hormones—adrenaline and cortisol.

CHAPTER EIGHT

Surviving School

No matter how hard Carmen studied, she just didn't understand her algebra homework. But she worked hard and managed to earn a B in the class. Carmen was relieved when she saw her grade, but when her parents looked at her report card, their faces grew stern. "A B-average in math?" her mother asked. "We expected better from you. This is unacceptable."

Some parents place a lot of pressure on their kids to get top grades in school. You may even be putting that same pressure on yourself. It can reach the point where you start to think "If I mess up on this test, my future is ruined." Of course, no one test will make or break your future plans—there will be opportunities to make things better if you fail to do well on one test or report. What can cause harm is when you have to deal with the stress that accompanies unrealistic expectations.

You need to be up-front with your parents if you think they are making unreasonable demands. Let them know you are doing your best and that they need to learn to accept you as you are.

However, if you are not working as hard as you could be, and are bothered by your grades, then you can take steps to improve them. Talk to your teachers about getting some extra help, look into tutoring possibilities, be sure you do your homework and turn it in on time, and try to improve your study habits.

Determine the study schedule that works best for you. You might find you're more productive if you do the easiest assignments first to get them out of the way, or you might prefer to save the easy stuff for later. Maybe you work well with partners, or maybe you're better off on your own. Only experience can determine what study routine works best for you. However, once you've hit on an effective formula, stick to it.

Dealing with bullies and fake friends. Another major school stressor can be bullies. The word *bully* doesn't refer only to the tough guy who beats up someone smaller than him. It can also be the girl who targets members of her own group. She mocks and insults those she claims to like, often convincing mutual friends to join in. If anyone calls her on that behavior, she insists she is not really serious. She's just joking.

This form of bullying is often called relational aggression. Its purpose is to hurt another person by damaging her ability to have friendships with others.

Tips for Improving Study Habits

- Do your best to find a quiet, well-lit place with as few potential distractions as possible (no TV, no phone).

- Ask your family not to disturb you unless there's an emergency.

- If you study in your room, don't risk falling asleep by sprawling on your bed.

- Make sure you have everything you need before you start to work.

- Take a break occasionally to collect your thoughts and to avoid fatigue—but keep it quick. Don't lengthen your break by getting involved in other activities, like watching TV or making a phone call.

- Avoid going online when working on the computer. It's easy to lose track of time or become involved in instant messaging with friends.

Relational aggression typically involves isolating the person, spreading false rumors about her, and name-calling.

Being put down or insulted is stressful. If you believe a friend honestly doesn't realize she's being mean, you need to let her know how you feel. If she laughs or insists you're lying, you're better off without her. A real friend would be shocked and upset to learn about your issue and willing to apologize. If she really seems sincere, then consider giving her the benefit of the doubt and accepting her apology.

If someone is bullying you, there are different ways to respond. Ignoring a bully can work, but sometimes that route is not always enough. A direct confrontation might be the best way to go. Try saying something like, "Look, I don't know what your problem is with me, but this isn't cool or funny and I think you'd better stop." Make eye contact and keep your voice level— don't whisper or shout. The bully might insult or dismiss what you've said at first, but at least you've proven you're not an easy target.

If you can't bring yourself to confront the bully— or you tried and it didn't work—you can tell your parents, a teacher, or guidance counselor what's happening. That solution is also the best plan if you fear for your physical safety. What's most important is that you take steps to stop the bullying behavior.

What to Do If You Are Being Bullied

1. Tell an adult.

2. Tell the bully to stop; then calmly walk away.

3. Do not fight back because you could also end up in trouble.

4. Lighten the mood and distract people by making a joke.

5. Make new friends and get involved in activities that interest you.

6. Don't blame yourself.

7. Be strong and believe in yourself—it's the bully who has a problem, not you.

From "Bring Bullying to an End," girlshealth.gov

CHAPTER NINE

Putting Pressure on Yourself

Veronica has a 4.0 GPA, is editor of the yearbook, plays varsity lacrosse, and serves on student council. After school, she takes piano lessons and volunteers with her youth group—after she's done her homework, of course. She goes out of her way to be friends with everyone. Veronica's teachers admire her, and her parents are proud. No one would ever guess that she averages four hours of sleep a night, plagiarizes to keep those grades up, and cries whenever she's alone.

Nobody's amazing at everything. But some girls, like Veronica, have a hard time accepting their own limitations. They are perfectionists, who stress over every mistake they make. Perfectionists obsess about or overemphasize doing everything correctly. In *Stressed-Out Girls: Helping Them Thrive in the Age of Pressure,* psychologist Roni Cohen-Sandler writes that perfectionists "equate being successful with being extraordinary ... [and] consider weakness in any area unacceptable." Too often such goals are unrealistic.

Ambition and drive are normally good things. But they can be very bad if taken too far. You've heard of athletes abusing steroids, students cheating on exams, and politicians lying—all of them jeopardizing their careers—in the name of achievement. If unchecked, perfectionism can lead to misery. Perfectionists have a hard time accepting when they have done a competent job. Too often they aim for the unattainable, extraordinary effort.

Negative thoughts. When you're your own harshest critic, you are also your own stressor. If you don't think the job you've done is good enough or

Are You a Perfectionist?

If you feel the burning need to excel, ask yourself the following questions—and do your best to be honest:

- Why do I want to improve or do well?
- When will I be satisfied with what I've accomplished?
- How will I react if I fall short of my expectations for myself?
- Can I handle coming in second or worse in a competition?

Self-Image Stressors

- I don't think I look very attractive.
- I'm not very good at sports or music or dance even though I practice a lot.
- I need to lose weight.

you're always comparing yourself to everyone else in your class, it is hard to be happy. And it's easy to feel stressed out.

If you keep telling yourself that you'll never be smart or athletic or talented enough, or that a situation is completely hopeless, you are piling on stress from within. Recognize that when you change your attitude, you will find relief from some of that stress. Try to take a more positive look at yourself. Make a list of your positive characteristics and of what you've done. Give yourself some credit, and don't let feelings of failure keep you down.

Problems with self-image. Most girls have no problem coming up with a negative comment about some aspect of their appearance. Something is wrong with their height, weight, nose, complexion, or hair— you name it.

During the teen years, when the body is undergoing the rapid changes of puberty, you may be especially sensitive about your looks. At the same time, you are being targeted in advertisements that say you have to be like impossibly pretty people. It's hard to have a positive self-image.

Just remember, the unpredictable changes your body is going through during puberty are completely normal. You're supposed to get taller, grow body hair, and gain weight while growing up. (And if you haven't yet, don't worry. It'll happen.) Try to keep in mind that your physical appearance isn't what should count in any relationship. Your real friends like you for who you are, not for how you look.

However, you may be finding faults with yourself that you really do want to change. If so, talk about your concerns with your parents or friends to see what they think. If they agree that you should lose some weight, for example, then do something about that goal. Contact your doctor to set up a weight-loss diet and exercise program, and then do your best to follow it. On the other hand, if your friends and family assure you that you don't need to make changes, listen to them.

CHAPTER TEN

Death, Loss, and Change

> *Jill's grandfather had been sick for many years. When he passed away last week, Jill was relieved that he was no longer in pain. But she also felt terribly guilty. What is wrong with me? she asked herself. How could I be happy that my grandfather is gone?*

Most changes and transitions cause a great deal of stress. One of the hardest—and most stressful—changes to deal with is the death of a close friend or family member.

Dealing with grief. When someone you really care about dies, you can experience agonizing emotions, including anger, shock, sorrow, and depression. Grief is one of the most difficult emotions to face, and the grieving process is grueling. One way to cope with your loss is to pay tribute to your loved one. Work through your grieving process by helping with a memorial service, putting together an album of favorite photographs, or creating a Web page that honors the deceased. The process of creating such remembrances can help you deal with your grief and stress. However, it will take time to work through your stages of grieving.

When friends grow apart. Yet another difficult change in life can be losing a friendship. Are you still as close to your favorite people as you always were? Maybe you've noticed a distance that wasn't there before. Sometimes, there isn't really any reason for friends to drift apart. It just happens during the process of growing up. As people learn more about who they are, they want new friends to reflect what interests them. And those interests can change as the years go by. If it seems like one of your best friends is hanging out a lot with someone else, it is natural to feel jealous. But try not to stress over the situation. Give the new person a chance, and maybe you'll end up liking him or her, too.

Moving. Sometimes you lose friendships because of something over which you have no control. It can be a major stressor when your family moves—you've lost familiar friends and surroundings. You have to make new friends and attend a new school. Feeling stress in this kind of situation is to be expected.

Five Stages of Grieving

First identified by psychiatrist Elisabeth Kübler-Ross in 1969, the five stages of grieving can apply to situations involving traumatic change (such as diagnosis of terminal illness), as well as the death of loved ones.

Denial—refusal or inability to understand the bad news; pretending that nothing has happened.

Anger—outpouring of feelings of anger, blaming self or others.

Bargaining—hoping that bad news isn't true or negotiating with others to prevent change.

Depression—sadness, regret, fear, uncertainty combined with beginnings of acceptance of what has happened.

Acceptance—ready to become actively involved in taking steps to move on.

Whether you're dealing with having moved from one place to another or simply changed schools, be patient and try to stay positive. If you're not happy with your new school right away, don't worry. Just give yourself time to settle in. It will get easier if you take advantage of the new opportunities your school offers. Go out of your way to talk to people in your classes. Join clubs that interest you. Just be true to yourself. That's the most effective way to make good friends who will be there for you.

Dealing with divorce. Life can also be stressful when parents don't get along or argue a lot. When their inability to get along ends in their breakup, you

Situation Stressors

- A close friend or family member has died.
- Someone in my family has been diagnosed with a serious disease.
- Money is tight since one of my parents was laid off.
- My family is moving.
- My parents are getting a divorce.

will find yourself dealing with a major family change—and a major stressor.

In 2005, out of every one thousand marriages in the United States, about seventeen ended in divorce. Many divorced couples have children who may have to move to new homes or choose between which parent to live with. Whether these kids are toddlers, teenagers, or adults, the changes resulting from divorce can be difficult to handle.

If you are one of these kids, it is natural for you to feel angry with one or both parents. Let them know if it bothers you when they say negative things about each other in front of you. If their behavior is stressful, you need to make it clear that you expect them to be civil with one another—for your sake.

Whenever you are dealing with change, it can help to share your feelings with friends and with others. Remind yourself that you're not alone, that you'll get through this, and that it's natural to feel stress and fear. But once you can recognize that things aren't going to go back to the way they used to be, you can begin to make plans to move on.

CHAPTER ELEVEN

When Stress Is Dangerous

> "My parents hate me."
> "I wish I was skinny like you; I'm such a pig."
> "This class makes me want to kill myself."

When people make negative comments about themselves they usually don't mean what they are saying. Most likely they are simply exaggerating a situation or even searching for a compliment by putting themselves down.

But sometimes when a person makes comments like these, they are signs that he or she is feeling overwhelmed and possibly spiraling out of control. If a friend has been suffering from chronic stress, he or she is at increased risk of developing serious emotional illnesses such as clinical depression and anxiety disorders.

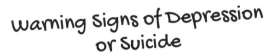

Warning Signs of Depression or Suicide

- Loss of interest in life
- Long-term feelings of sadness
- Weeks of constant anger and bad moods
- Severe changes in eating habits
- Unexplained injuries
- Negative comments about self-worth
- Giving away belongings

Clinical depression is usually diagnosed when a person's strong feelings of sadness and helplessness last for more than two weeks. He or she will have difficulty in thinking and concentrating and may have significant changes in appetite and sleep needs. Clinical depression interferes with the person's ability to connect with others and function in any environment—at work, at school, or at home.

Some anxiety in life is perfectly normal—who hasn't suffered from a bit of stage fright before giving a speech? However, when anxiety is excessive, it can be harmful. Anxiety disorders make the tasks of everyday life seem overwhelming and impossible. In many cases, it's hard for sufferers to function in social settings. Physical symptoms typically include heart palpitations, migraines, and panic attacks.

Clinical depression and anxiety disorders are linked to self-injury (such as cutting) and suicide. Yet, both mental health disorders are treatable with the proper medication and professional counseling. A friend with issues may not want others to know there is a problem. But remember, by getting help for your friend, you're doing the right thing. People suffering from depression and anxiety disorders are at risk of causing harm to themselves. According to the U. S. Centers for Disease Control and Prevention, suicide is the third leading cause of death among fifteen- to twenty-five year-olds.

If you think your friend may be exhibiting signs of depression, an eating disorder, drug use, or self-

When You Should Ask for Help

- You have been feeling sad for more than two weeks.
- Your grades are dropping.
- You worry a lot.
- You easily get moody or angry.
- You feel tired all the time.
- You get a lot of headaches, dizziness, chest pain, or stomach pain.
- You feel bored all the time and are less interested in being with friends.
- You are thinking about using alcohol or drugs to try to feel better.
- You are thinking about hurting yourself.

Adapted from "A Teen's Personalized Guide for Managing Stress: When to Turn for Help," American Academy of Pediatrics

injury, or is having suicidal thoughts, you need to get help. Tell a trusted adult (a parent, school counselor, your family doctor, or religious leader) about your concerns. Or call one of the hotline numbers listed on page 63.

CHAPTER TWELVE

Managing Your Stress

Would you want to live in a world without stress? For most people, the answer is no. What would motivate people to get anything done in a completely stress-free world? The shock to the system that stress provides often gives momentum needed at the right moment.

Stress can result from good things, too. Not all stressors are unhappy or frustrating situations. Stress can result from emotions like extreme excitement and anticipation, as well as from anger and humiliation. The intensity of your emotions can directly affect the amount of stress you feel.

Have you ever spent all evening getting ready for a dance you'd looked forward to for weeks? Did your face break out the day before? Did a run in your stocking make you panic? Did your stomach churn every time you looked at the clock? Maybe so, but more likely than not, it was all worth it once you got there and started having fun.

Many experts refer to stress from negative sources as distress and stress from positive sources as eustress (literally "good stress"). Other moments of eustress that you may have experienced include performing in a play or concert, planning a party, going on a date, getting ready for a vacation, or playing a competitive sport. Eustress can give you the focus that allows you to perform at your very best.

Still, you need to recognize that too much stress—whether from positive or negative stressors—can be bad for you. If you let it, eustress may keep you working too long on something that interests you and keep you awake so late at night that you don't get needed sleep. And any stress that lasts a long time can lead to health problems.

Whether your stress is part of positive emotions (interest or excitement) or negative ones (anger, humiliation, or sadness), it is important to stay on top of it when you can. Just remember that perspective is the magic word in stress management. Almost no mistake will ruin your life. You can gain control of the situation. When you find yourself feeling stressed out about something, remind yourself, as many times as necessary, that it's not the end of the world. Life will go on.

Recognize your limitations and set reasonable goals. Be ready to prioritize: What needs to get done sooner? What will take longer? Do you need more resources? Can you break something into smaller steps? Everything can't always get done perfectly, and it isn't fair to expect perfection from yourself or anyone else.

Learn from the past. After a period of stress is over and the stressor is taken care of, see if there's anything you can learn from the experience. Staying up late at night to finish a report might teach you not to put off large projects until the last minute. There might even be a bright side that will become clear later—for instance, a fight with your friends in which you fear losing their friendship can help you realize how important they are to you.

Know when to ask for help. There's no shame in asking for help from others when you feel stressed out. At the same time, being private about your

You can't always change the way other people think and act, but you do have the power to change the way you react to them.

Tips for Reducing Stress

- Keep a positive attitude.
- Accept that there are events that you cannot control.
- Be assertive instead of aggressive. "Assert" your feelings, opinions, or beliefs instead of becoming angry, defensive, or passive.
- Learn and practice relaxation techniques.
- Exercise regularly. Your body can fight stress better when it is fit.
- Eat healthy, well-balanced meals.
- Get enough rest and sleep. Your body needs time to recover from stressful events.
- Don't rely on alcohol or drugs to reduce stress.
- Seek out social support.
- Learn to manage your time more effectively.

"Tips for Reducing Stress," *WebMD,* December 2006

stress is fine, too. Everyone has different needs and preferences. Try to figure out what yours are.

Throughout your life, you will have to deal with stress. There will be bullies or difficult people. There will be disappointments, changes, and losses. Brooding over your problems, your failures, or other issues won't really accomplish anything. In fact, your negative emotions will only make things worse.

But when you take positive steps to deal with the stress in your life, you can make a difference. Look to support from family and friends. They can help you take the steps needed to solve stressful conflicts or deal with change. At the same time, be positive about yourself and what you can accomplish. That positive attitude will ensure that you stay on top of your stressors and reduce your stress.

Books

Bernstein, Ben. *A Teen's Guide to Success: How to Be Calm, Confident, Focused.* Familius, 2013.

Hipp, Earl. *Fighting Invisible Tigers: Stress Management for Teens.* Minneapolis, Minn.: Free Spirit Publishing, Inc., 2008.

Miller, Allan R. *Living With Stress.* New York: Checkmark Books, 2010.

Internet Addresses

American Academy of Pediatrics: A Teen's Personalized Guide to Managing Stress

http://www.aap.org/stress/buildresstress-teen.htm

TeensHealth: Stress

http://kidshealth.org/teen/your_mind/emotions/stress.html

Hotlines

National Alcoholism and Substance Abuse Information Center Helpline

1-800-784-6776

National Suicide Prevention Lifeline

1-800-273-TALK (8255)

INDEX

Stressed-Out Girl? Girls Dealing With Feelings